The Renaissance for Kids

A Captivating Guide to a Period in the History of Europe Following the Middle Ages

Table of Contents

INTRODUCTION

Have you ever wondered who painted the Mona Lisa? Or why there are so many different churches today? Or even if the sun goes around the Earth? People were asking similar questions during the Renaissance! The Renaissance was a time in European history when people rediscovered ancient texts and began practicing modern science. They discovered new ways to make art and began asking hard questions about the world around them. We're still asking some of those questions today!

But how did the Renaissance begin? And why does it matter today? The Renaissance was over 500 years ago, but it was a time filled with amazing discoveries, powerful popes, and art so beautiful that people today still travel thousands of miles to see it. The Renaissance was fueled by powerful merchants who brought wealth into Europe, and it grew because of inventions like the printing press. The people of the Renaissance dreamed big dreams. They imagined helicopters and tanks hundreds of years before the technology existed. They discovered gravity and invented calculus. The Renaissance completely changed how we live our lives today.

This book has everything you need to learn about the wealth of art and learning that came from the Renaissance. Both students and parents will enjoy reading this fun, up-to-date history of this critical time period. Get ready to sail in and discover how the Renaissance has shaped the world as we know it today.

Chapter 1: What Started the Renaissance?

The **Renaissance** was a time of big change for the people in Europe. It changed the way they thought and lived. "Renaissance" literally means "rebirth" in old French. Ancient ideas that had been lost during the Middle Ages were reborn in Europe. It changed many things, like **art, architecture, science,** and **philosophy**. Philosophy is the study of what and how we think. Everyone sees the world differently, so there are lots of different philosophies!

The Renaissance was a time filled with creativity and learning. Before that, Europe was in the **Middle Ages**. When the **Roman Empire** fell in 476 CE, Europeans lost much of the security they needed to continue learning and creating. People stopped reading and writing because they were worried about surviving—and, eventually, they forgot how to read. The only people who could read in the Middle Ages were important church leaders. Even kings couldn't always read! That meant that books were usually kept at **monasteries**, where monks lived. The monks spent a lot of time reading and copying books because there wasn't a way to print them yet.

Life during the Middle Ages was really hard. Most people worked long hours and were afraid of attacks from groups like the Vikings. They thought life was supposed to be hard, so they didn't try to improve it. Most people didn't have much money or a way to learn new things, so they didn't know any other way to live.

That all changed during the Renaissance, which started in **Italy**. Italy is the country on the southern side of Europe that looks like a boot.

Map of Central Europe

https://commons.wikimedia.org/wiki/File:1915_Strategic_Map_of_Central_
Europe_showing_the_International_Frontiers_Prepared_in_the_War_College_Division,_
General_Staff,_War_Department.jpg

Today, Italy is one country. But, back then, it had lots of little countries called **city-states** that were always competing with each other. **Florence** was one of those cities, and it became very powerful. It wasn't strong because it had a great army. It was powerful because it was really good at business and banking. From Florence, the Renaissance quickly spread all over Europe!

The Renaissance was a huge change for the people in Europe. But what made it happen? Historians think the Renaissance started for several different reasons.

One thing that started the Renaissance was the invention of the printing press. Around 1450, **Johannes Gutenberg** invented the **printing press**. This might not seem like a big deal to us now, but it was revolutionary back then. Before the printing press was invented, books had to be copied by hand. It took a lot of time, and that meant books were expensive. Not many people could afford books. After Gutenberg invented the printing press, that all changed. He got the press to work so well that he could even print large books like the Bible and sell them cheaply. Suddenly, many people could afford books, and they began learning and thinking for themselves.

They didn't just print the Bible. They printed anything they thought was interesting, including things written by the ancient Greeks and Romans. For most of the Middle Ages, those writings were lost. When they were found, they were printed on the printing press so lots of people could read them. These ancient writings were even translated into different languages! Not a lot of people could read Latin or ancient Greek. After reading ancient works, including the Bible, more people started thinking for themselves.

Another reason the Renaissance began was the increase of trade. The Europeans liked a lot of things from Asia. To get those things, they had to join trade routes like the **Silk Road**. It was called the Silk Road because one of the things people traded was **silk**, a very soft and expensive fabric.

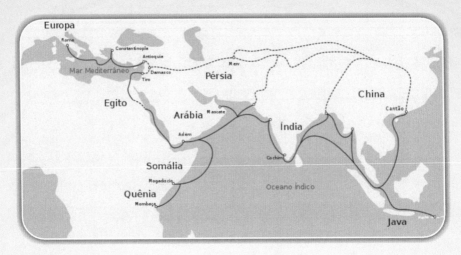

Map of the Silk Road.

The Silk Road stretched from China all the way to Europe. Merchants traveled in large groups and had to always beware of bandits. Trading with Asia helped European merchants become wealthy. They traveled on land with camels and over the ocean with ships to buy and sell luxury goods.

Renaissance-Era Trade Ships

By bringing money back into Europe, merchants helped to start the Renaissance. At the time, a common way to show your wealth was to hire artists. A wealthy merchant would become the **patron** of an artist who would make paintings, sculptures, and even buildings for the merchant. Artists competed with each other to get wealthy patrons. This competition fueled the Renaissance because it motivated artists to find new and better ways to make art. It started in Florence, but soon, the city-states were also competing with each other to see who had the best artists. Everyone tried to be the best artist they could be, and this made the art even better.

Another reason the Renaissance began was the **Black Death**. The Black Death was a pandemic caused by the **bubonic plague**. It started in Asia in 1347 and came to Europe on the trade routes, killing millions of people. It was very scary for the people of Europe because they didn't know what caused it. They also didn't have any medicine to help people get better. Today, we know that the bubonic plague was partially spread by fleas that lived on rats. The cities were very dirty, so there were lots of rats. They didn't know that back then, and people were very afraid.

At first, people asked the church to help them because they thought the plague was a punishment from God. When the church couldn't stop it, some people began looking for answers in other places. The Black Death killed between 75 million and 200 million people in just a few years. Europe lost a lot of workers, but the Black Death helped start the Renaissance by moving people around Europe and making them think about other things than just the church.

There are lots of different reasons the Renaissance began, but the final reason we will look at is the fall of **Constantinople**. Constantinople was the capital of the **Byzantine Empire**. This empire had a long history of being connected to the Roman Empire but survived its fall. While the rest of Europe fell into the Middle Ages, the Byzantine Empire kept going in the east. Its people still created art and read the writings of the ancient Greeks and Romans.

The fall of Constantinople.
https://commons.wikimedia.org/wiki/File:Fall-of-constantinople-22.jpg

In 1453, Constantinople fell to the **Ottoman Empire**. When this happened, many people fled to western Europe—and took their ideas with them. These ideas were new for the Europeans. With all these ideas and changes coming to Europe, the people experienced a rebirth of art, learning, and thinking that changed their way of life forever.

Chapter 1 Challenge Activity

Can you identify the correct word for each description and put it in the crossword puzzle?

ACROSS

2. The people that wealthy merchants would sponsor
4. The pandemic caused by the bubonic plague that killed millions of Europeans
8. The man who invented the printing press
9. The study of thinking about what and how we think

DOWN

1. The trade route from Asia to Europe
3. How the European merchants became wealthy
5. The capital of the Ottoman Empire
6. The city-state where the Renaissance began
7. Means "rebirth" in Old French

Chapter 2: Renaissance Ideas and Values

The Renaissance was a time when people looked at many different ideas and **philosophies**, or ways of thinking. The way we think influences the way we act and the way we see the world. Many of these philosophies actually came from the ancient Greeks, so they weren't new at all! All these ways of thinking were new to the Europeans, though, because they had been lost during the Middle Ages.

Let's look at four popular philosophies during the Renaissance. By looking at these ideas, we'll understand more about how the Renaissance changed Europe and brought it out of the Middle Ages.

Humanism

Humanism is the idea that people have certain rights simply because they are people. This was very different from the thinking of the Middle Ages. During the Middle Ages, people believed that value came from a set of rules. These rules applied to all people and situations and were usually given by religion. Following the rules and not thinking about yourself too much was very important.

During the Renaissance, humanism rejected the idea that all value has to come from a set of rules. Instead, all people were valuable and should be allowed to get a good education. People who believed in humanism thought people should learn all about ancient literature and art. This area of education is called the **humanities** because it looks at what makes us human.

Humanists, or people who believed in humanism, were very focused on art. They thought that beauty was linked to virtue and value, so a lot of their art celebrated people's beauty. This philosophy was eventually also connected to logic and science, but it started with a celebration of art.

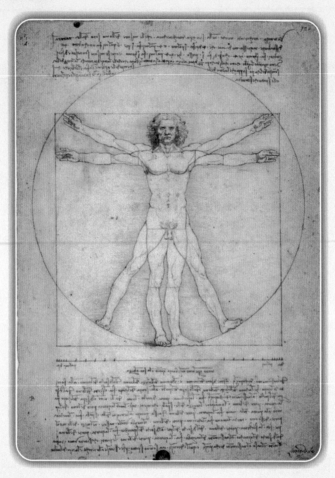

The Vitruvian Man by da Vinci.
https://pixabay.com/fr/illustrations/leonardo-da-vinci-l-homme-de-vitruve-1125056/

In modern times, some people say that the humanists rejected religion. While this may be true of humanism today, it was not true during the Renaissance. Humanists during the Renaissance did not entirely reject religion. They just wanted to look at other places to find value as well. For them, religion was part of a person's life but shouldn't be the only thing in a person's life. Religion can provide some guidelines for making life better for people on Earth. Humanists believed that was good because people deserve good lives just because they are human.

Many historians believe the first humanist of the Renaissance was **Petrarch**. He was an Italian scholar and poet who lived in the 1300s. He wasn't the first person to think up humanism, but he helped introduce it back into Europe. Because of this, he is often called the "Father of Humanism."

Skepticism

Skepticism is the idea that people should carefully think about statements before believing them. This doesn't mean skeptics don't believe anything—they just believe people should think deeply about things.

Skepticism first started in Ancient Greece. Some of the traveling teachers were very good at talking through logic, but every statement depended on something else. For some people, this was really frustrating. They said that these teachers had not found the truth because nothing they said could stand by itself. These people were called **skeptics**. They believed in critical thinking and thought that these traveling logic teachers had not told the truth.

During the Renaissance, skepticism focused on thinking about ideas carefully. Skeptics thought that ideas that relied on someone else's authority to be true were not very strong. They also didn't think complicated philosophies were good. For the Renaissance skeptics, this philosophy was really a habit of questioning everything they heard and using logic to find answers. Instead of just accepting something was true because the king or the church said it was true, the skeptics would think about what truth is and how to find it.

Different people reached different decisions, and these decisions sometimes included religion! Later on, skepticism would be part of the **Reformation**, when people began asking questions about the Christian religion and making changes to it. Several different groups broke away from the Catholic Church and started their own churches because they had decided the Catholic Church did not have the whole truth. Whether they were right or not, they used skeptical thinking learned during the Renaissance to reach their conclusions.

Individualism

Individualism is the idea that one person is more important than a group. Each person has certain freedoms that shouldn't be taken away and should only depend on themself. Every person is special and should be recognized for their differences.

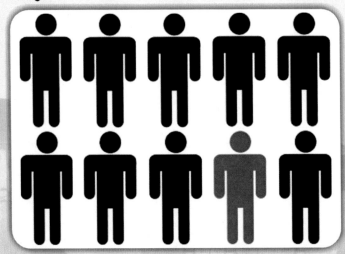

Individualism: The concept of the individual.

This philosophy was a big change from the beliefs of the Middle Ages. In the Middle Ages, people believed that your identity was **corporate**, or tied to the group you belonged to. So, if you were attending school, your identity was a student. Other examples of identities were serf, priest, or Roman. Everyone stayed in their identified group. Innovating or thinking outside the box was not encouraged.

During the Renaissance, people began to create their own identities. People pulled away from the crowd and showed what made them special. Because they didn't have to fit in with a group anymore, they were able to stretch and reach their potential. One example of the benefits of individualism was **Leonardo da Vinci**. He did not have to stick to the expectations of one group, so he did a variety of things, like painting and inventing. Da Vinci even drew a plan for a helicopter! He couldn't have done that if he had been limited to taking his identity only from one group.

Individualism allowed people to be creative. They could play with ideas and art forms, which helped art to get better. Artists also began signing their work and taking pride in their accomplishments. The Renaissance was a celebration of the individual because people believed that the individual could do great things.

Secularism

Secularism is the idea that life should be lived well while on Earth. The word "secular" means "of this world." This world contrasts with Heaven, and the ideas of secularism were very different from the ideas of the Middle Ages. Before, people believed that life was supposed to be hard. The church told them that life had to be endured so that they could go to Heaven. People wanted to go to Heaven, so they focused on the afterlife instead of life on Earth.

During the Renaissance, people saw that life was getting better. There were more economic and political opportunities, and they were excited. People began living life on Earth for its own sake. Of course, they had not forgotten Heaven or their religion, but now they were interested in the world around them.

Secularism is easiest to see in Renaissance paintings. Artists used more details and made sure these details were true to life. Plants, animals, nature, and people all looked more realistic. Painters also began creating art that wasn't directly tied to the Bible. In fact, some of their art wasn't inspired by Christianity at all! They were busy exploring the world around them and finding other reasons to enjoy life.

All four of these philosophies were tangled together during the Renaissance. Some people believed more than one. Together, they helped pull Europe out of the Middle Ages and made people think about how to achieve great things during their lifetime.

Chapter 2 Challenge Activity

Can you match the philosophy to its definition?

Humanism	The idea that one person is more important than a group
Secularism	The idea that people have certain rights simply because they are human
Individualism	The idea that people should carefully think about statements before choosing to believe them
Skepticism	The idea that life should be lived well while on Earth

Chapter 3: The Renaissance in Italy

The Renaissance started in Italy. At that time, Italy was very wealthy, so it was easiest for new art and ideas to start there. One of the most important cities during the Renaissance was **Florence**.

In the 1100s, Florence was a very small town. It wasn't important at all! But, like other Italian city-states, Florence became powerful through business. Florence had two main areas of trade. The people of Florence traded **wool** and worked in **banking**. Both of these jobs were great for making money. Wool was needed for clothes, and banking was important for keeping money moving.

As Florence got more powerful, the merchants also became more powerful. One of these families was the **Medici** family. The Medici worked in banks and traded wool, so they were in the perfect position to become wealthy. They even had their own bank called the Medici Bank, which had branches all over Europe. The Medici family earned so much money in business that they also became an important part of the Florence government. Many leaders in Florence were from the Medici family during the Renaissance. In fact, they ruled Florence until 1737!

The first major government leader from the Medici family was **Cosimo de' Medici**. He lived during the early 1400s and became the **Gran Maestro** of Florence in 1434. That means that he became one of their leaders. Cosimo was a very good leader and took care of Florence.

Cosimo de' Medici.

Another important member of the Medici family was **Lorenzo de'**
Medici, Cosimo's grandson. He was also called **Lorenzo the**
Magnificent. Lorenzo ruled Florence during the height of the
Renaissance, and he was also a good leader for Florence.

One reason Lorenzo is remembered so well is that he was a patron
of the arts. A **patron** is a person who pays artists to make art.
Having art around your home was a way to show how wealthy you
were. If you wanted a really impressive piece of art, you had Io pay
an artist to make it. This required a lot of money, so not everybody
could be a patron. Artists would compete with each other to get the
richest patrons. The Medici family was the richest family in Europe,
and they used their money to help the Renaissance. They funded a

lot of the most famous artists. You may have heard of some of them, such as Michelangelo, Donatello, and Leonardo da Vinci.

Lorenzo de' Medici.
https://commons.wikimedia.org/wiki/File:Lorenzo_de%27_Medici-ritratto.jpg

The Medici family didn't just sponsor artists. They also gave money to **scientists** and **scholars**. Scientists were trying to figure out the world around them, including the solar system. One of the scientists they supported was the famous astronomer Galileo Galilei.

Scholars were more interested in ancient writings. They wanted to read all the ancient Greek and Roman texts, but finding them was expensive. The Medici family paid for scholars to find the texts and make them easier for others to read later.

The Medici were more than just patrons. They were also strong politicians. Even though they weren't royalty, they became powerful enough to marry royalty. A few members of the family even became

popes in the Catholic Church. The pope was one of the most powerful people in Europe, so this was a big deal.

One of the most famous Medici popes was **Pope Leo X**. He lived from 1475 to 1521 and became the pope in 1513. Leo X is most famous for funding many artistic projects and making Rome an important cultural city for the Renaissance. The **Vatican**, where the pope lives, was well decorated, and Leo X spent both his and the church's money to pay artists, such as Raphael, to beautify it. He even paid architects to build beautiful churches and improve the streets of Rome. When he died, he left behind beautiful art for the world to enjoy and 600,000 ducats (gold trade coins) of debt for the next leaders to handle.

Pope Leo X.
https://commons.wikimedia.org/wiki/File:Raphael_-_Pope_Leo_X_with_two_cardinals.jpg

Before Leo X became pope, the Catholic Church was led by **Pope Julius II**. He also commissioned a lot of art, like the painting of the **Sistine Chapel** by Michelangelo, but art wasn't Julius' main focus. Instead, he was known as "the Warrior Pope." Julius increased the papal (pope's) military and even led a couple of military campaigns. It might seem a little strange that the Catholic Church had a military. During this point in history, the church was more than just a religious group. It also had a lot of land and a lot of political influence. The church used its military to protect its power and collect even more land, just like the Italian city-states.

Pope Julius II.
https://commons.wikimedia.org/wiki/File:Pope_Julius_II.jpg

Both Pope Julius II and Pope Leo X spent a lot of money, and they weren't the only church leaders who did this. The church had also become more interested in getting and keeping power. As the

Renaissance introduced new ideas to the people of Europe, they began accusing the Catholic Church of being corrupt. Popes were selected because of who their families were, not because they tried hard to be religiously moral. They used the church's money to fund public and private projects. While the buildings and art were beautiful, the church needed more money to pay for it all. So, they started selling **indulgences**. An indulgence was a pardon from punishment for sin. The Catholic Church believed that after people died, they would be punished in **Purgatory** for the bad things they had done before being allowed to go to Heaven. To raise money, the church told people these pardons would get them or their family members into Heaven faster.

During the Renaissance, people began applying humanism to their Christianity, and this started a change in Christianity called the **Reformation**. People wanted all the corruption in the Catholic Church to stop, and their different ideas about what religion should be led to the creation of **Protestant** churches. The Catholic Church did a lot of work to fix its problems in the **Counter-Reformation**, but these different groups within Christianity still exist today.

Chapter 3 Challenge Activity

Can you answer the following questions in one or two sentences?

1. **Who were the Medici?**

_____

_____

_____

2. **Why did people think the Catholic Church was corrupt?**

_____

_____

_____

3. **What was a patron?**

_____

_____

_____

4. **How did the Medici help fund the Renaissance?**

_____

_____

_____

5. **How long did Pope Leo X reign?**

_____

_____

_____

Chapter 4: Leonardo da Vinci

Leonardo da Vinci is one of the most famous painters of the Renaissance. He had a natural talent for painting, and he was always trying new techniques to improve his work. Although da Vinci was famous as a painter, he was also a **Renaissance man**. A Renaissance man is a person who is good at many different things. Leonardo da Vinci did a lot of things during his life. He was a painter, an inventor, a botanist, an anatomist, and a sculptor. That doesn't even name everything he did! He really loved learning, so he was constantly exploring and experimenting.

Image of da Vinci.
https://commons.wikimedia.org/wiki/File:Leonardo_di_ser_Piero_da_Vinci.jpg

Leonardo da Vinci was born in a small town in Italy called **Vinci** in 1452. He began painting when he was still a kid, so when he was fourteen years old, his father got him an apprenticeship in

Florence. An **apprenticeship** is when a student learns how to do a job while working at the job. You can still get apprenticeships today for some jobs, and they are important for learning new skills.

Da Vinci's apprenticeship was with Verrocchio, a good artist in Florence. After learning with Verrocchio for about six years, Leonardo da Vinci started working on his own. He painted for many years, but only fifteen of his finished paintings are still around today. Two of his most famous paintings are the *Mona Lisa* and *The Last Supper*.

The *Mona Lisa* is one of the most famous paintings in the world. Leonardo da Vinci started working on it in 1503, and it took him several years to finish. He created it using oil paints on a panel of wood. The painting is of a woman named Lisa Gherardini (jer-ar-de-ni). She was the wife of Francesco del Giocondo (jo-con-do), a silk merchant from Florence. It's a small portrait, but it is special for several reasons. First, Lisa is not painted the way portraits were usually painted. People typically wore their best clothes and jewelry for a portrait because it was a special occasion. Lisa wore a dark dress and a thin veil. Even stranger, she is smiling. People usually didn't smile for portraits.

The *Mona Lisa* is a unique portrait, but da Vinci made it more original by using the **sfumato technique** (sfo-ma-do). This painting technique uses glazes to create soft shadows. "Sfumato" is the Italian word for "smoke" since the soft shadows can look like smoke in a painting. The whole painting is mysterious because no one really knows why *Mona Lisa* is smiling. Its mysterious air has captured the imagination of people throughout the centuries, beginning with **King François I** (fran-swa). He bought the painting from da Vinci in 1518, and it has belonged to France ever since. You can see the *Mona Lisa* for yourself today. It is on display at the Louvre Museum in Paris, France. The portrait is kept in a protective case to protect it from humidity—and anyone who might want to steal it.

Mona Lisa.

Another very famous da Vinci painting is *The Last Supper*. Unlike the *Mona Lisa*, *The Last Supper* is a **fresco**. This is a specific style of mural painting. Traditionally, the artist uses watercolors directly on wet plaster. As everything dries, the paint attaches to the plaster, and the painting becomes a permanent part of the wall.

Leonardo da Vinci did something different with his fresco painting. Instead of painting on wet plaster, he painted on dry plaster by prepping the area with gypsum and then painting with tempera and oil. It allowed him more time to be precise with the details and colors. Unfortunately, that also means the mural has needed to be restored several times. His experimental technique was not stable, but his painting was so popular that it is still known all over the world.

The Last Supper shows the last meal Jesus ate with his disciples before he was arrested. Every character has a natural reaction in the scene, which helps make the painting look even more realistic. When da Vinci finished, everyone agreed that it was a masterpiece. This painting is still on the original wall in Milan, Spain, where you can see it today.

The Last Supper.

Leonardo da Vinci had a lot of unfinished paintings, as well, like *The Adoration of the Magi*. There are a few reasons he didn't finish several of his works. First, he was busy and often put off his work. Procrastinating meant that he never finished some projects. Second, he experimented with new techniques a lot. Not all of these new ways to paint were good. Some of them were even a disaster! Da Vinci could not sell his failed experiments, so they weren't finished, either.

When he wasn't painting, Leonardo da Vinci was learning about the world around him. He wrote down a lot of his findings in his **notebooks**. He made over 13,000 pages of notes, and many of his notebooks are in museums today. They are filled with interesting notes, drawings, and inventions. His inventions were centuries ahead of his time. He had sketches to build a tank, a hang glider, and even a helicopter!

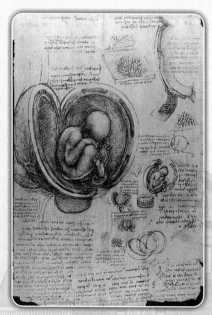

Notes from da Vinci's notebooks.
https://commons.wikimedia.org/wiki/File:Da_Vinci_Studies_of_Embryos_Luc_Viatour.jpg

He also had a lot of drawings of the human body. He drew bones, organs, and muscles and tried to be as accurate as possible. He learned all about the human body because he was allowed to **dissect** bodies after people had died. Leonardo da Vinci's research helped other artists create more accurate-looking people in their paintings and sculptures.

Da Vinci's notebooks are also remarkable because he wrote them entirely in **mirror writing**. Mirror writing is when you write everything backwards. Some people think that da Vinci wrote backwards because he was trying to keep his work a secret. But this probably isn't true. Leonardo da Vinci was left-handed, which made it hard to write normally with a quill and ink. A quill was a large feather with a sharpened end, and the ink could take a long time to dry. He didn't want to smear the ink, so he used mirror writing instead.

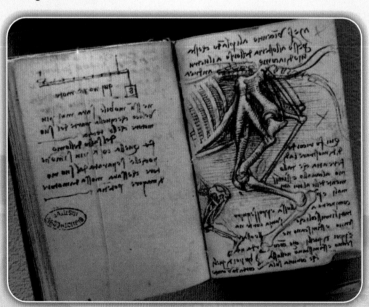

Mirror writing and drawing of bones.
https://www.flickr.com/photos/cogdog/3097567215

During his life, Leonardo da Vinci gave us some of the most famous paintings in the world and did a lot of scientific research. Without his work, the Renaissance would not have made as many scientific discoveries—and the world would be a sadder place without the mysterious smile of the *Mona Lisa*.

Chapter 4 Challenge Activity

Can you color the picture below as if you were Leonardo da Vinci? Feel free to experiment with different colors as you work!

Leonardo da Vinci (1452-1519) - The Last Supper (1495-1498)
Leonardo da Vinci, CC0, via Wikimedia Commons
https://commons.wikimedia.org/wiki/File:The_Last_Supper_Line_Art.svg

Chapter 5: Michelangelo

Michelangelo was another very famous artist during the Renaissance. He is famous for both his paintings and his marble sculptures. Although Michelangelo lived around the same time as Leonardo da Vinci, they actually weren't friends! They had different opinions about how art should be created, but they were still respectful of each other.

Michelangelo was born on March 6, 1475, in **Caprese**, a city near Tuscany. His father worked in the government, and soon after Michelangelo was born, he and his family moved to Florence. When he was a kid, he loved watching the painters and exploring all the beautiful art in Florence. When he turned six years old, his father tried to send him to school, but Michelangelo wasn't interested in school. He wanted to be an artist.

When he was thirteen, Michelangelo got his wish. He got an apprenticeship with the painter **Domenico Ghirlandaio** (do-min-e-co gil-an-di-o). Ghirlandaio's workshop was very busy, so Michelangelo learned a lot of things, like how to paint frescos and make sculptures. He only learned from Ghirlandaio for a year before he was sent to learn more about carving sculptures from **Bertoldo di Giovanni** in the **Medici gardens**. (The Medici family was so rich and powerful that they had a school where famous artists and philosophers could meet and learn from each other.) Michelangelo learned a lot about sculpture and even began making sculptures of his own called **reliefs**. A relief is a flat piece of material like wood or marble that has raised figures.

Michelangelo began his career as a sculptor and artist when he was still a teenager. Can you imagine making famous art before you're an adult? You would have to work very hard to build the skills you need!

He worked for the Medici family in Florence and a few other Italian cities for several years. He was already very good. Some people have said that Michelangelo could see a finished sculpture in a block of marble. It helped him plan and create beautiful art. Eventually, the pope heard about Michelangelo and asked him to come to Rome. Michelangelo was only twenty-one years old.

While Michelangelo was in Rome, he made several very important pieces of art. One of them was the *Pietà* (pe-ay-ta). The French ambassador asked him to make it, and Michelangelo started sculpting it around 1497. The statue shows the **Virgin Mary** crying over Jesus' body after his crucifixion but before his burial. In the Catholic faith, this is a very important moment.

At the time, it was unusual to have two figures together in one statue. Michelangelo carved the two figures to be one piece. He also displayed his skill at making marble look like fabric. This is very difficult to do. He used a drill and careful carving to create natural-looking folds and creases, just like fabric. The faces also display real emotions, and they are beautiful. Michelangelo wanted to show their connection with the divine.

Michelangelo was proud of the *Pietà*. It was the only art piece that he ever signed. During the Renaissance, more artists began signing their work, but they still didn't sign everything. The statue became famous immediately. Lots of artists talked about how great it was, and it helped make Michelangelo famous. You can still see the *Pietà* in Saint Peter's Basilica at the Vatican in Rome, Italy.

The Pieta.

Another famous statue that Michelangelo carved is *David*. He moved back to Florence in 1499 and started carving this statue in 1501. It took him three years to finish it! The piece of marble that he was given was very tall and thin. Other sculptors had tried to make a sculpture from it, but it was too hard for them. Some people didn't think Michelangelo would be able to do anything with it, either, because the marble block was damaged.

Michelangelo worked on the statue for three years in secret. When he finally showed his work to everyone, they were all impressed. The statue is over five meters tall, or over **fifteen feet**! It is full of energy because Michelangelo sculpted the muscles and tendons carefully. He took care to keep his work as natural and realistic as possible. David's eyes convey his determination to take down Goliath. The realism is part of why this statue made Michelangelo even more famous.

When Michelangelo finished *David*, Florence put it in the **piazza**. A piazza is a public square, so many people saw it. It became a symbol of Florence's freedom.

You can still see *David* in Florence, Italy. The original statue has been moved into the Academy of Fine Arts, but there are a few copies of the statue throughout the city. Many people think the *David* is Michelangelo's best statue because it is nearly perfect.

Although Michelangelo was famous for his statues, he was also a **Renaissance man** (like da Vinci). In 1508, Pope Julius II asked Michelangelo to paint the ceiling of the Sistine Chapel. The pope had to work hard to convince him. Michelangelo didn't think he was a painter, but he finally agreed to do it. It took him four years to paint the whole ceiling because it was so big --roughly 141 feet long by 43 feet wide. He had to paint the ceiling while lying down on a scaffold. Can you imagine how difficult that was? Michelangelo had to plan his painting very carefully so that he could paint it once he got up to the ceiling. When he was finished, there were nine main scenes from Bible stories and over 300 people. Every single person looks unique, just like people in real life.

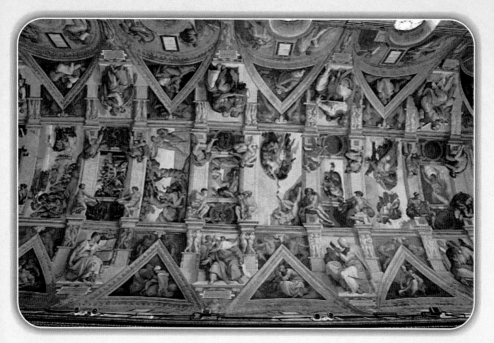

The Ceiling of the Sistine Chapel
https://commons.wikimedia.org/wiki/File:Sistine_Chapel_ceiling_photo_2.jpg

The nine scenes are all from the Old Testament. Three show the **Creation story**, three show the **Fall of Man**, and the last three show the story of **Noah and the Flood**. The most famous scene on the Sistine Chapel ceiling is the *Creation of Adam*. It shows God reaching out to Adam to finish creating him.

Michelangelo finished the Sistine Chapel ceiling before November 1, 1512, and it has been famous ever since. You can still visit it today and see all the art on the walls and ceiling. Michelangelo did not paint all of the Sistine Chapel, but he did paint the ceiling and the wall fresco showing *The Last Judgment*. It is also very large and shows Michelangelo's skill at painting realistic-looking humans.

Michelangelo worked closely with many high-ranking officials throughout his life, including the Medici family and powerful church leaders. He even designed St. Peter's Basilica, but he didn't live long enough to complete it. Michelangelo died on February 18, 1564 and was buried in Florence.

Michelangelo's art is world-famous. For years, many artists tried to copy his techniques. He gave us some of the most memorable art from the Renaissance that has changed the course of history. He showed us that art can reveal the true emotions of humanity and impact people hundred of years later.

Chapter 5 Challenge Activity

Can you fill in the blanks?

Pieta	Sistine Chapel	sculptor
Rome	Renaissance	

Michelangelo was a famous painter and _____ during the Renaissance. He worked in a lot of Italian cities, like _____ and Florence. One of his most famous statues is the _____. Some of the marble is carved to look like fabric, which is really hard to do. Michelangelo also painted the ceiling of the _____ because the pope asked him to. It was really hard because he had to paint while lying down. Still, Michelangelo worked really hard to be one of the best artists in the _____, and he became one of the most well-known artists in history.

Chapter 6: Great Discoveries

The Renaissance was more than just a time of amazing art. People were also working hard to understand the world around them. **Humanism** helped people become more interested in science. Part of humanism was reading the writings of the ancient Greeks and Romans, who left lots of writings about science. Their work made people ask questions about the world.

The people of the Renaissance also believed that the world around them worked under strict rules. They believed everything was orderly, so they wanted to discover what that order was. Their curiosity drove a lot of the scientific discoveries during the Renaissance. They looked all around them, looking at things like rainbows, water, and the night sky.

People have always been curious about the stars. They have been looking up at them since before people began writing down history. During the Renaissance, people began asking different questions about the stars and **astronomy**, which is the study of space. One of the important astronomers during the Renaissance was **Nicolaus Copernicus**. He was born on February 19, 1473, in Prussia. (Today, the land that was Prussia is part of Germany.)

Copernicus was a Catholic priest, but he had several hobbies. He liked studying things like math and astronomy. While observing the night sky, he came up with a new way of looking at the universe. Before, everyone believed in a **geocentric** model of the universe. This means they thought the Earth was the center of the universe: it stayed still, and everything else revolved around it. Copernicus didn't think that was right. He came up with a **heliocentric** model of the universe. He said that the sun was actually the center of the universe. All the planets revolved around it, even the Earth! He wrote a book called *On the Revolutions of the Heavenly Spheres* in 1532, but he did not publish it until 1543. Copernicus died two months after his book was published.

Copernicus never proved his theory that the sun was the center of the universe, but his work helped other astronomers during the Renaissance think about the universe differently. They began asking questions about the old way of looking at the world and thinking they could find a better explanation.

Portrait of Nicolas Copernicus.

Another great astronomer from the Renaissance was **Galileo Galilei**. He was born in Pisa, Italy, on February 15, 1564. His family was full of musicians, but Galileo thought he wanted to be a doctor.

He went to school to study medicine but didn't get very far. Instead, he decided that science was more interesting.

Galileo became a teacher and spent a lot of time doing **scientific experiments**. He also spent time trying to write math formulas for the science he was discovering. One of his famous experiments tested if two things would hit the ground at the same time if they had different weights. He went up the **Tower of Pisa** to drop two balls off it. Even though they weighed different amounts, they hit the ground at the same time!

Galileo's biggest discovery came in astronomy. He had heard of Copernicus' theory and thought he could prove it. In 1609, Galileo went to Holland because he heard they had invented a **telescope**. He then made a better one for himself. He discovered moons around Jupiter, sunspots, and craters on the moon. His telescope wasn't powerful enough to prove Copernicus' theory, but he wrote about how it must be true in his book *Dialogue Concerning the Two Chief World Systems*.

Galileo Galilei.

Galileo's book upset some of the powerful people in the Catholic Church. They made him withdraw his theories because they were different from the church's beliefs at the time. The church also put him under house arrest for the rest of his life.

Other scientists did not have the same problems with the church that Galileo did. Science and the church were not really opposed to each other. **René Descartes** was an important scientist and philosopher. As a scientist, he was one of the people who helped form the **scientific method**. Before the Renaissance, people didn't really do scientific experiments. The scientific method allowed people to find new facts through structured experiments. Descartes also developed math. He focused on defining shapes and finding equations for them. His work was so important that it helped another great scientist: Isaac Newton.

Isaac Newton is famous as the person who discovered gravity. He was born on January 4, 1643, in Woolsthorpe, England. He grew up with his grandparents and spent a lot of time alone. When he was nineteen years old, he went to Cambridge University. He eventually became a math professor there as he worked on his great math and science theories.

Legends say Newton discovered the concept of gravity while watching apples fall out of an apple tree. We don't know if that's true, but Newton did figure out that gravity is what makes things fall down. Newton was very interested in **physics**: the science of how things move. During the Renaissance, this was still a very new area of study. People didn't have a lot of background knowledge to help them. Isaac Newton changed that. He developed three **laws of**

motion to help people see how everything moved. He also created a new kind of math called **calculus**. This math is still used today by scientists and engineers. Isaac Newton wrote down all his theories in his book *Mathematical Principals of Natural Philosophy*.

Isaac Newton.

The Renaissance was full of scientific discoveries and inventions. The **telescope** and the **microscope** were both invented and improved during the Renaissance. People were learning how to make lenses, which helped people see the world around them better. Mechanical clocks were also invented, which helped people keep time better.

There were also scientific advances in warfare, such as the **cannon** and the **musket**. Both ended the warfare of the Middle Ages, pushing Europe into the modern age.

Science during the Renaissance was very important. Many people thought up new ways to look at the world and invented new things to make life easier—like the wrench and the screwdriver. Not everyone was right about everything, but that is part of the learning process. What really matters is that these scientists worked hard to help us understand the world better, and we still use many of their ideas and inventions today.

Can you put these inventions in timeline order?

- **Newspaper – 1605**

- **Military telescope – 1590**

- **Astrolabe – 1551**

- **Telescope – 1609**

- **Mechanical clock – 1410**

Chapter 7: Astonishing Architecture

The art in the Renaissance was more than just painting and sculptures. **Architecture** was another kind of art that developed during the Renaissance. Architecture is the way that buildings are designed. Some buildings are meant to be very pretty, and that's what makes buildings art.

Architects, or people who design buildings, created a lot of buildings during the Renaissance. They took inspiration from the ancient Greeks and Romans. Just like other parts of history, architecture has gone through a lot of changes. Before the Renaissance, **Gothic architecture** was very popular. It had a lot of stonework and looked **irregular**. Architecture during the Renaissance was very different. Because Renaissance architects drew inspiration from ancient building styles, they used columns and liked to create symmetry. They took the parts of ancient architecture they liked and shaped them to fit their needs.

When you look at Renaissance-era buildings, you'll see a few features that almost all Renaissance architects used. They are what characterized the movement. Many buildings had **arches** or **domes**. An arch is half a circle. When it's built correctly, it can provide structural support. A dome is half a sphere. The architects placed domes on top of buildings because they looked impressive. Domes were also hard to build, so building them showed the architect's skill.

Renaissance arch.

Renaissance architects also used **columns**. One type is called a **Doric column**. These columns are very simple and do not feature much carving. In fact, the tops of Doric columns are usually plain. Another type is called an **Ionic column**. These columns are more decorated than Doric columns. They always have a special decoration at the top that looks like two scrolls.

Architects also designed their buildings to have order. They wanted everything to be geometrically perfect and have symmetry. This means that they organized their buildings carefully using mathematical proportions. A **proportion** is when you look at part of something in relation to the whole thing. For Renaissance artists, everything had to fit into proportions so the parts looked like they belonged together. The **golden ratio** was very important. Architects used this special proportion to make their buildings appear beautiful, and many artists still use it today.

The Renaissance architects also usually designed buildings into squares or rectangles because those are good shapes for **geometry**. Geometry is a type of math that focuses on shapes. The intent was to show rationality and clarity, which were very important qualities in the Renaissance. In a way, the main ideas of the Renaissance also influenced how architects built their buildings. They used a lot of natural light in their buildings to symbolize how light and knowledge were returning to Europe.

Like other parts of the Renaissance, this new architecture started in Florence. One of the first creators of Renaissance architecture was **Filippo Brunelleschi** (fi-lee-pow broo-nuh-leh-skee). In 1419, he was commissioned to build a large dome for **Florence Cathedral**. It was the biggest dome built since the **Pantheon** in Ancient Rome was built 1,500 years before! People had forgotten how to build domes that big, so Brunelleschi had to invent how to do it. It took over four million bricks to build the dome, and the gold ball on top weighs almost two tons by itself! Brunelleschi's technique for lifting heavy objects high up in the air was used by other architects to build other domes across Europe.

Florence Cathedral

Brunelleschi worked on Florence Cathedral for most of his life, but he also worked on other buildings. One of them was the **church of San Lorenzo**. This church looks very different from churches of the Middle Ages, which had pointy arches on their windows. The church of San Lorenzo had round arches on its windows and had arches and columns. This church was designed to look orderly and symmetrical. It showed other architects how different the Renaissance style was going to be, and other churches across Europe followed Brunelleschi's example.

Sadly, Brunelleschi never finished this church. The outside still shows its rough bricks, so no one knows what it was really supposed to look like. The church of San Lorenzo is missing its **fa ade**. During the Renaissance, a lot of buildings had a fa ade. This is a special front that was added onto buildings to help make them look more symmetrical. The bricks were like the bones of the building, but the faade was supposed to be the only part you could see on the outside. Some faades used **ashlar masonry**. This special kind of stonework uses stones of the same size and texture. They are carved to look exactly alike and then put closely together to form a wall. It makes the whole building look even cleaner and more symmetrical.

There are many other Renaissance buildings. One of them is the **Palazzo Vecchio** (vec-i-o). This was Florence's city hall. A lot of the Palazzo Vecchio was built during the Middle Ages, which is why the outside looks different from other Renaissance buildings. Inside, the building was renovated by the Medici family in the 1500s. They turned the city hall into their private home. Many of the rooms were redone to fit the Renaissance style, so there are numerous Renaissance paintings inside the building.

Palazzo Vecchio.

Another is the **Basilica of Santa Maria Novella**. This church is one of the most important in Florence. It was also started during the Middle Ages, so the inside does not look like other Renaissance churches. However, the fa ade was completed during the Renaissance by **Leon Battista Alberti**. He used lots of geometrical shapes to make the building look like the other Renaissance buildings that were being built. He even had Renaissance paintings added to the inside of the church!

Basilica di Santa Maria Novella.

Renaissance architecture didn't stay in Italy. It spread quickly across Europe to places like France, England, Germany, and even Russia. It didn't stay the same as it traveled across Europe, though. It changed as it met other local traditions, so every area had a unique version of Renaissance architecture.

In England, there was a lot of Renaissance architecture because **Inigo Jones** brought it back to England. Inigo Jones lived from 1573 to 1652 and was an important architect. He designed the **Queen's House** in 1616 and the **Banqueting House of Whitehall** in 1619. England still constructed its buildings in the style of the Middle Ages, with lots of **turrets** and **mullion windows**. These new buildings had the same clean lines and lots of symmetry, so the styles mirrored each other to create beautiful buildings.

The English are a good example of how European countries handled this new architecture. Many architects followed Inigo Jones' example in later buildings, but they combined traditional architecture with the ideas of Renaissance architecture. The English kept their turrets and mullion windows but made everything more symmetrical. They also added more carving, like the Italians did. They used Renaissance architecture to make their own architecture that was both modern and traditional.

Chapter 7 Challenge Activity

Can you match the picture of the building with its name?

St. Peter's Basilica

Florence Cathedral

Basilica of Santa Maria Novella

Palazzo Vecchio

Chapter 8: The Birth of Philosophy

The Renaissance was a time full of new ideas. This meant that there were also a lot of new philosophies. Everything that people in Europe thought was changing. The people began questioning freedom of choice and **morality**, which is the difference between good and evil. Some of these questions led to problems in the church. People began asking questions about life and death and wondering if they even had any freedom of choice. If they didn't, that might mean God had already planned everything they would do. This idea is called **predestination**. During the Renaissance, people did not find a lot of solid answers to these questions, but they did begin thinking differently about the world around them.

Humanism was a big part of philosophy, too. Remember: humanism believed that everyone had inherent worth. It also focused more on the present world instead of the afterlife. This change influenced philosophy, making it more focused on people and the pursuit of knowledge.

There were many different philosophers during the Renaissance. One of them was **René Descartes**. (You might remember him from Chapter 6.) He was a scientist, but he also spent a lot of time thinking about philosophy. He has been called the "**Father of Modern Philosophy.**" His ideas are important for understanding modern philosophy, starting with the Renaissance.

He introduced **continental (European) rationalism** in the 1600s. Rationalism is the philosophy that people can think through everything logically. People shouldn't use their emotions to make decisions. People who practice rationalism think that emotions can't be trusted. Descartes believed that the world was real—and that he could prove it. He started with a very famous statement: "I think; therefore, I am." It means that because a person thinks, they must exist.

Proving existence was important to Descartes. A popular philosophy before he entered philosophy was called **skepticism**. Skepticism is a philosophy that believes that people have to question everything. In extreme forms, some people question whether or not we actually exist! Descartes used rationalism to show that we must exist. He said the world had to exist, too, and he believed that he could prove God exists. He used his mind to find answers, which is what made him a **rationalist**.

Rene Descartes.

Another important philosopher was **Lorenzo Valla**. He was born in 1407 and died in 1457. He did not invent a specific philosophy. Instead, he spent his life criticizing the traditional philosophies that most people believed at the time. He showed that tradition wasn't always true and argued that it was good to question popular ideas.

At heart, Valla was a humanist. He spent a lot of time making the ancient philosophers easy for others to understand. He translated and sometimes simplified famous authors like Aristotle. He also wrote many books. The most famous one is called *Elegances of the Latin Language*. It was a textbook about correct vocabulary and sentence structure in Latin. **Latin** is the language that the ancient Romans wrote in, and many ancient Greek texts were translated into Latin. Humanists needed to be able to understand Latin to read the ancient texts that they were rediscovering. His Latin textbook was the first one, and it was very popular.

Between all his jobs and writings, Valla found plenty of time to question the popular ideas of the time. Mostly, these ideas were held by the church, so Valla spent a lot of time questioning church leaders. The church thought you had to live a hard life to be morally right, but he believed that people could live good lives and be comfortable at the same time. He also thought that some of the church's teachings were not as historical as they said they were. He even said that the **Apostle's Creed** was not written by the Apostles. The church leaders were so upset that the **Inquisition** investigated him. Valla was saved from death by King Alfonso.

Valla helped make the way for other humanists to question the ideas around them. He helped move Europe away from the Middle Ages' ideas and into the Renaissance's ideas. Even though his questions were sometimes hard, his work is important to understanding the Renaissance.

Lorenzo Valla.
https://commons.wikimedia.org/wiki/File:Lorenzo_Valla_aport011.png

Marsilio Ficino (fa-seen-o) was another important humanist philosopher who lived from 1433 to 1499. He believed the ancient texts were very important, and he was the first person to translate all of Plato's works into Latin from Greek. Other people had translated some of Plato's writings, but Ficino was the first person to translate all of them himself.

Ficino spent some time working for the Medici family. When Cosimo de' Medici decided to start a school of philosophy just like Plato's, he chose Ficino to be its leader. Ficino believed that the writings of many of the ancient philosophers had pieces of truth in them. He thought people should be properly educated, which meant they needed to read as many different texts as possible and think carefully about what they were reading. He also thought philosophy was related to **theology**, which is the study of God. Ficino was very religious, and his beliefs were an important part of how he understood the world around him. So, studying philosophy from a book should be combined with good moral living. Ficino was an important academic leader in Florence for several years, but he became a priest later on. Throughout his life, he wrote about his ideas to his friends. Those letters are where we get most of Ficino's ideas today.

Marsilio Ficino.
https://commons.wikimedia.org/wiki/File:Marsilio_Ficino.jpg

Another important Renaissance philosopher was **Niccolò Machiavelli**, who lived from 1469 to 1527. He had a lot of jobs during his life: poet, musician, politician, and philosopher. Machiavelli is most famous for writing a book called *The Prince*. In this book, he talks about what it takes to be a strong leader of a country.

Before Machiavelli wrote this book, most people believed that the way to be a strong leader was to be a good person. Leaders who lived virtuous lives would also have a peaceful and strong government. This might make sense at first, but when you think about it, it isn't always true. Sometimes a leader is a very good person but still has a terrible time running the country.

Machiavelli noticed this, too. He said that being a good person is not how people can ensure their right to rule. Instead, all that matters is having and keeping power. Power is the only way that leaders keep their authority, so they should do anything to get and keep power. Leaders can use fear and violence to control their people if necessary.

Some people think that Machiavelli didn't really believe what he wrote in *The Prince*. It's very different from his other books. He possibly wrote it for the Medici family because he was trying to convince the family to like him after they took back power in Florence. If so, it didn't work, but the book has been popular ever since.

He wrote several other books and has been called the **Father of Modern Political Philosophy**. That's a big name! It means that he started the practice of thinking critically about how to run governments. He didn't just look at policy and laws. He also looked at how the way people think causes them to make political decisions.

Machiavelli changed how we think of government, which allowed people to start being more critical of their leaders.

Portrait of Niccolò Machiavelli.

There are many different Renaissance philosophers, but the last one we will look at is **Petrus Ramus.** He was a French philosopher who lived from 1515 to 1572. Ramus was very popular during his life because he wanted to change how people read ancient authors like **Aristotle.** He was a humanist, so he believed that interpreting these ancient texts was very important.

During the 1500s, governments were changing. They were becoming bigger and more powerful. Ramus tried to influence the education system to better match the new governments.

Ramus believed that logic was not a way to argue. Instead, it was a tool. Anything could be argued using logic. This was not a new idea, but Ramus wrote books that made it a popular idea. His work also helped bring humanism into other parts of Europe, which was important to the growth of the Renaissance. He used his job as a philosophy professor to spread his ideas, even though some of his fellow teachers did not think his ideas were original.

Chapter 8 Challenge Activity

Can you fill out this crossword puzzle?

ACROSS

3. The question of good and evil
5. The book that said strong leaders just need power
6. The author of The Prince
8. The belief that people have inherent value

DOWN

1. One of the languages that ancient texts were written in
2. The idea that God controls every action you take
4. The ancient author who Ficino translated
7. The French philosopher who said logic was a tool for arguments

Chapter 9: The Printing Press

The printing press was essential to the Renaissance. Without this amazing invention, the Renaissance would have taken longer and been very different.

Johannes Gutenberg is credited with inventing the printing press. However, he was not the first person to print. People in China had been printing for hundreds of years before Gutenberg was born. Gutenberg invented the printing press in Europe and created the European version of **movable type**.

Before Gutenberg invented the printing press in Europe, creating books was really hard. People had to write books by hand. They would also decorate the book with drawings and fancy writing. Can you imagine trying to copy a whole book? It would take a lot of time and energy! Also, most people couldn't write. You had to be very well educated to know how to write. Both of these reasons made it difficult to produce books—and only wealthy people could afford to buy them.

In some places, people were starting to learn how to print, but all the letters for a page had to be carved on a block and then stamped onto the page. This also took a long time, so books produced like this were not any cheaper.

Johannes Gutenberg was born around 1398 and died in 1468. We don't know a lot about his childhood, but we do know that he lived in Germany. His father was a goldsmith. When Gutenberg grew up, he saw how hard it was for people to get books, so he decided to do something about it. While living in France in 1440, he began experimenting with the current printing technology, but he did not have a complete printing press until 1450. By then, he was back in Germany. His new invention was called the **Gutenberg Press**.

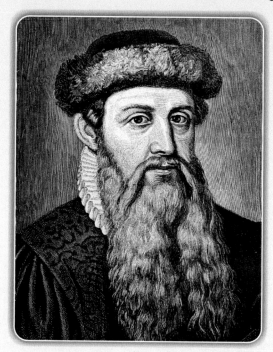

Portrait of Gutenberg.
https://commons.wikimedia.org/wiki/File:Gutenberg.jpg

This printing press was different from anything that had come before it. Gutenberg decided to replace the wooden blocks other people used for printing with individual metal letters. He had to make enough metal letters to spell out a whole page, but stacking all the letters together was much faster than carving each letter into wood. Also, because each letter was individual, he could reorganize the letters he had to make any page he wanted. This was called **movable type**. While it might not sound like a big deal to us today, it was revolutionary in Europe at that time. It completely changed the printing business because it allowed Gutenberg to print faster and save money.

However, using metal letters had a problem. All printing ink at that time was designed to stick to wood, not metal. Gutenberg had to invent his own kind of ink to make sure his metal letters could print words. Inventing a new printing press made Gutenberg create all kinds of new things to make it work faster.

The rest of the frame was made out of wood. Gutenberg even installed a **paper press** to make sure the paper was flat before going in for printing. (Printing is hard if the paper is folded or curling.) The paper press was designed like an old wine press. The paper was first put between two pieces of wood. A long handle turned a giant screw that pushed the top piece of wood onto the paper, flattening it. The paper press used a lot of pressure!

15th-century printing press.
https://commons.wikimedia.org/wiki/File:Medieval_printing_press.jpg

Gutenberg started his press printing little things like pamphlets and calendars. He became really famous when he decided that he wanted to print the Bible. Gutenberg printed the Bible in 1452 with Johann Fust's help. His version was called the **Gutenberg Bible**. It was the first time the Bible had been printed like this. Before, Bibles were written out by hand, and a priest might need a whole year to copy one. This meant Bibles were rare. Gutenberg's printing press made it much easier for middle class people to have one. He printed around 200 Bibles, some of which are still around today. His press could produce about 250 pages an hour, which is over 1,000 pages a day! For a long time, the Gutenberg Press ruled the printing industry.

Statue of Gutenberg.

Gutenberg was so successful that other people were soon following him. They set up their own Gutenberg presses, and Europe was flooded with printed books that more people could afford. The printing press first came to Italy in 1465, and by 1470, many printers had successful businesses. German printers spread across Europe, taking the Gutenberg press into places like France, Spain, and England.

There were now so many books that people began sharing ideas and education faster than they had ever been shared before. This may sound really exciting to us, but some of the powerful people in Europe were worried. They knew that if people started thinking for themselves, they might decide they didn't want the current leaders to stay in power.

The church tried to stop people from printing and reading anything that went against church beliefs. Pope Alexander VI even threatened to kick people out of the church if they printed things without the church's approval. This was called **excommunication**, and it was a really big deal. Being excommunicated meant that you wouldn't be part of the church anymore. In some areas, you wouldn't even be allowed to talk to anyone who was part of the church! People also believed that you wouldn't go to Heaven if you were excommunicated because the priest wouldn't forgive your sins. For the people of the 1500s, being excommunicated was a very scary threat.

Even with the threat of the church's anger against all of these new books and ideas, there was no stopping the Gutenberg press. It allowed people to encounter new ideas by giving them access to cheaper books. In 1605, the first newspaper was printed. The ordinary person could now get information faster and across larger distances, which would change the world forever. Without the Gutenberg press, many of the ideas of the Renaissance would not have traveled as far or been as influential because people would not have been able to read about them.

Chapter 9 Challenge Activity

Imagine that you lived before Johannes Gutenberg invented his press. Try writing the opening page of a book below! You can make one up or copy from your favorite book.

Chapter 10: Consequences and Impact

The Renaissance was the gateway from the Middle Ages to the modern world. It had immediate consequences in Europe. People began to think for themselves and question traditions. They looked at the world around them and called for changes, especially in the church. In the Middle Ages, the only church was the Roman Catholic Church. But, as people began to ask questions, the **Reformation** began. People wanted the old and corrupt practices removed from the church, and some of these people started their own churches. The split between Catholicism and Protestantism began because of the Renaissance. Today, these other branches of Christianity are called **denominations**.

The Renaissance also eventually led to the **Enlightenment** and the **Scientific Revolution**. The Enlightenment was a time of philosophy. People built on the philosophy of the Renaissance to think even more differently. The Scientific Revolution was a time in Western history when people invented lots of different machines and processes. They learned many new things about science, but they could not have done so without the work done by scientists during the Renaissance.

The scientific method was defined during the Renaissance, and it continues to shape how we practice science today. Science is focused on rationally testing theories with experimentation and observation. No question or theory should be rejected without first testing it. That way, we have rational explanations for everything. Natural curiosity and the desire to find truth through experiments come from the Renaissance and have defined modern scientific discoveries.

Students practicing science.

There were other consequences of the Renaissance throughout history. The Renaissance began because Italian traders grew wealthy enough to pay artists to create art and scholars to study ancient texts. As money continued to come in, Europe developed a **middle class**. This group of people were not royalty but had enough money to live comfortably. This class would later become more powerful and want a voice in the government.

Because of the Renaissance, European governments also changed. During the Middle Ages, almost everyone lived under the **feudal system**. This was a system for dividing land. If you had a lot of land, you could allow people to live on it. They would give you money every year and have to do things for you—such as fighting on your side in a battle or tending your crops. In return, you had to protect them from raiders. It was a useful system, but it kept everyone very separated.

The Renaissance ended the feudal system. **Monarchies** began to rise as a national form of government. A monarchy is when a king or queen runs the government. Kings and queens became very strong leaders, and the countries we know today began to form.

As the middle class grew stronger and countries developed, people began looking for other ways to make their fortune. Trading was important to making money, so people began exploring. They were looking for better ways to get to Asia, but along the way, they found the **New World**. Soon, people were setting sail to explore the New World. European influence in the Americas was an important part of their development. Many countries in the Americas today would be different if the Renaissance had not encouraged people to explore.

The expansion of printing.
Internet Archive Book Images, No restrictions, via Wikimedia Commons
https://commons.wikimedia.org/wiki/File:The_printing_trades_(1916)_(14742723976).jpg

The middle class also had a big interest in education. People wanted to learn all they could about everything. This was aided by the invention of the **printing press**. Books were an important part of education during the Renaissance, and people relied on the printing press to spread the new ideas of the Renaissance. Today, we still rely on the printing press, even though there is a wealth of information on the Internet. Books continue to be an important part of learning, and we have found ways to make printing presses even faster. They now run with electricity and print thousands of pages a day!

During the Renaissance, reading change how people saw the world. Reading continues to be an important part of our lives. It is one of the main ways we find and learn new information. Whether we are reading to learn or to be entertained, it still has the same effect today.

Modern-day telescope.

The Renaissance was also filled with inventions that we still use today. People began to think critically about the world around them, and as they were investigating, they invented things to make their jobs easier. Some of those things, like **microscopes**, help us see very small things. We still use microscopes today! The people of the Renaissance also invented things like **telescopes**, which help us see things that are very far away. While few of our modern inventions look like those used during the Renaissance, they still laid the foundation for many of the discoveries we have made today.

Perhaps the most important impact of the Renaissance is the reminder that we can look to both the past and the future to better our lives. The people who made the Renaissance so important in history wanted to make the future better, but they didn't ignore the past. It's sometimes easy to think that people from history didn't know as much as we do. Sometimes, that's true. But, in many ways, people from history knew a lot more than we do now. We can still learn from them. The Renaissance focused on using the past to make the future better. They built on the foundation laid by ancient people, and they changed the world. As we move forward into the future, it's good to take a moment to look back. The Renaissance changed the course of history, and it continues to impact how we look at the world today. There's a lot we can learn from the Renaissance, and this book has only scratched the surface of this world-changing time in history.

Chapter 10 Challenge Activity

Can you answer the following questions about the Renaissance?

1. **Which artist painted the Sistine Chapel?**

    a. Michelangelo　　　　b. Leonardo da Vinci　　　c. Donatello

2. **What invention allowed people better access to books?**

    a. Microscope　　　　b. Clock　　　　c. Printing press

3. **How wrote The Prince?**

    a. Rene Descartes　　　b. Machiavelli　　　c. Lorenzo Valla

4. **Who argued that the Earth traveled around the sun?**

    a. Galileo　　　　b. Copernicus　　　　c. Both

5. **Why did Leonardo da Vinci use mirror writing?**

    a. He was left-handed　　　b. He was writing in secret

    c. He never went to school

6. **Which family was the most powerful in Italy during the Renaissance?**

    a. The da Vincis　　　b. The Medici　　　c. The Gutenbergs

7. **Which philosophy believed that humans could achieve anything and that people should study ancient texts?**

    a. Humanism　　　　b. Skepticism　　　　c. Secularism

8. **Where did the Renaissance start?**

    a. America　　　　b. Italy　　　　c. France

9. **What does the word "Renaissance" mean?**

    a. Fancy art　　　　b. Rebound　　　　c. Rebirth

10. **What were the consequences of the Renaissance?**

    a. Less reading　　　b. Forgetting the past　　　c. Neither

Answer Key

Chapter 1:

ACROSS
2. Artists
4. Black Death
8. Johannes Gutenberg
9. Philosophy

DOWN
1. Silk Road
3. Trade
5. Constantinople
6. Florence
7. Renaissance

Chapter 2:

Humanism

The idea that people have certain rights simply because they are human

Secularism

The idea that life should be lived well while on Earth

Individualism

The idea that one person is more important than a group

Skepticism

The idea that people should carefully think about statements before choosing to believe them

Chapter 3:

Answers for this section will vary. Here are some sample answers.
1. Who were the Medici?

The Medici family was a powerful family in Italy. They ran banks and were very wealthy. They were able to support many artists as patrons.

2. Why did people think the Catholic Church was corrupt?

People thought the Catholic Church was corrupt because it was becoming more interested in having power. The pope fought in wars to get land and power. He also spent the church's money on private and public projects, which made the church poor. The church started selling indulgences to make more money, but some people thought that was wrong.

3. What was a patron?

A patron was a wealthy person who paid artists to make sculptures and paintings. They also paid scientists and scholars to study the world around them. Patrons were very important during the Renaissance.

4. How did the Medici help fund the Renaissance?

The Medici were important patrons. They paid for artists to make art and scholars to do research. They got their money from banking and trading wool.

5. How long did Pope Leo X reign?

Pope Leo X reigned from 1513 to 1521. That is eight years.

Chapter 5:

Michelangelo was a famous painter and sculptor during the Renaissance. He worked in a lot of Italian cities, like Rome and Florence. One of his most famous statues is the Pieta. Some of the marble is carved to look like fabric, which is really hard to do. Michelangelo also painted the ceiling of the Sistine Chapel because the pope asked him to. It was really hard because he had to paint while lying down. Still, Michelangelo worked really hard to be one of the best artists in the Renaissance, and he became one of the most well-known artists in history.

Chapter 6:

- Mechanical clock – 1410
- Astrolabe – 1551
- Military telescope – 1590
- Newspaper – 1605
- Telescope – 1609

Chapter 7

St. Peter's Basilica

Florence Cathedral

Basilica of Santa Maria Novella

Palazzo Vecchio

Chapter 8:

ACROSS

3. Morality

5. The Prince

6. Machiavelli

8. Humanism

DOWN

1. Latin

2. Predestination

4. Plato

7. Ramus

Chapter 10:

1. a. Michelangelo
2. c. Printing press
3. b. Machiavelli
4. c. Both
5. a. He was left-handed
6. b. The Medici
7. a. Humanism
8. b. Italy
9. c. Rebirth
10. c. Neither

If you want to learn more about tons of other exciting historical periods, check out our other books!

ANCIENT GREECE
FOR KIDS

A CAPTIVATING GUIDE TO GREEK HISTORY, FROM THE MYCENEAN CIVILIZATION AND THE TROJAN WAR THROUGH THE GOLDEN AGE OF PERICLES TO THE HELLENISTIC ERA AND ROMAN CONQUESTS

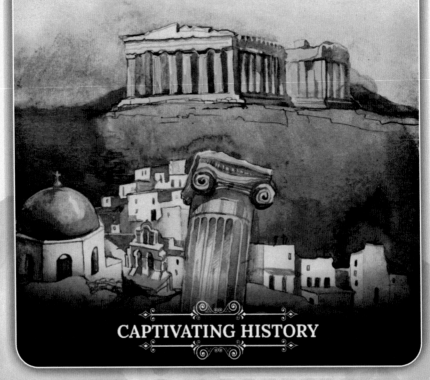

CAPTIVATING HISTORY

Bibliography

"Ancient China: The Silk Road." *Ducksters*. Technological Solutions, Inc. 2022. https://www.ducksters.com/history/china/silk_road.php

"Art History and Artists: Michelangelo." *Ducksters*. Technological Solutions, Inc. 2022. https://www.ducksters.com/biography/artists/michelangelo.php.

"Ashlar Masonry: Definition, Art History & Types." *Study.com*. Last updated November 2021. https://study.com/academy/lesson/ashlar-masonry-definition-art-history-types.html.

"Biography: Galileo Galilei." *Ducksters*. Technological Solutions, Inc. 2022. https://www.ducksters.com/biography/scientists/galileo_galilei.php.

"Biography: Johannes Gutenberg." *Ducksters*. Technological Solutions, Inc. 2022. https://www.ducksters.com/biography/johannes_gutenberg.php.

"Biography: Leonardo da Vinci." *Ducksters*. Technological Solutions, Inc. 2022. https://www.ducksters.com/biography/leonardo_da_vinci.php.

"Biographies for Kids: Isaac Newton." *Ducksters*. Technological Solutions, Inc. 2022. https://www.ducksters.com/biography/scientists/isaac_newton.php.

Britannica, T. Editors of Encyclopaedia. "Petrus Ramus." *Encyclopedia Britannica*. 1 January 2022. https://www.britannica.com/biography/Petrus-Ramus.

---. "Printing Press." *Encyclopedia Britannica*, 1 October 2021. https://www.britannica.com/technology/printing-press.

---. "Santa Maria Novella." *Encyclopedia Britannica*. 6 December 2017. https://www.britannica.com/topic/Santa-Maria-Novella.

"Defining the Renaissance by Its Values." Accessed May 2022. https://www.vanderbilt.edu/olli/class-materials/Session_4_Presentation_Italian_Renaissance.pdf.

"Ceiling." *Musei Vaticani*. Accessed June 2022. https://www.museivaticani.va/content/museivaticani/en/collezioni/musei/cappella-sistina/volta.html.

"Fall of Constantinople Facts for Kids." *Kiddle Encyclopedia*. Last modified 16 July 2021. https://kids.kiddle.co/Fall_of_Constantinople.

"From the 'Mona Lisa' to 'The Wedding Feast at Cana': The Salle des États." *Louvre*. Accessed June 2022. https://www.louvre.fr/en/explore/the-palace/from-the-mona-lisa-to-the-wedding-feast-at-cana.

"Galileo Facts for Kids." *Cool Kid Facts*. Accessed June 2022. https://www.coolkidfacts.com/galileo-facts-for-kids/.

Hamlin, William M., and Gianni Paganini. "Skepticism in Renaissance Thought." *Oxford Bibliographies Online*. Oxford University Press. Last modified 29 November 2017. https://www.oxfordbibliographies.com/view/document/obo-9780195399301/obo-9780195399301-0371.xml.

"House of Medici Facts for Kids." *Kiddle Encyclopedia*. Last modified 16 July 2021. https://kids.kiddle.co/House_of_Medici.

"Humanism." *Academic Kids Encyclopedia*. Accessed May 2022. https://academickids.com/encyclopedia/index.php/Humanism.

"Humanism." *Britannica Kids*. Encyclopedia Britannica. Accessed May 2022. https://kids.britannica.com/students/article/humanism/274981.

"Humanism Facts for Kids." *Kiddle Encyclopedia*. Last modified 16 July 2021. https://kids.kiddle.co/Humanism.

"Individualism." *Academic Kids Encyclopedia*. Accessed May 2022. https://academickids.com/encyclopedia/index.php/Individualism#:~:text=From%20Academic%20Kids,self%2Dreliance%20and%20personal%20independence.

Jarus, Owen and Jessie Szalay. "The Renaissance: The 'Rebirth' of Science & Culture." *Live Science*. Future US Inc. 11 January, 2022. https://www.livescience.com/55230-renaissance.html.

"Leonardo da Vinci Facts for Kids." *Kiddle Encyclopedia*. Last modified 9 April 2022. https://kids.kiddle.co/Leonardo_da_Vinci.

"Leonardo Di Ser Piero Da Vinci." *Leonardo da Vinci: The Complete Works*. 2017. https://www.leonardoda-vinci.org/.

"Lorenzo Valla." *Stanford Encyclopedia of Philosophy*. Last updated July 2021. https://plato.stanford.edu/entries/lorenzo-valla/.

"Marsilio Ficino." *Stanford Encyclopedia of Philosophy*. Last updated September 2017. https://plato.stanford.edu/entries/ficino/.

"Marsilio Ficino Facts for Kids." *Kiddle Encyclopedia*. Last modified 20 March 2022. https://kids.kiddle.co/Marsilio_Ficino.

"Medici Family: Origins and History." *The Medici Family*. Accessed June 2022. http://www.themedicifamily.com/.

"Michelangelo's David." *Florence Museum*. Accessed June 2022. https://www.florence-museum.com/michelangelo-david.php.

"Michelangelo Facts for Kids." *Kiddle Encyclopedia*. Last modified 9 April 2022. https://kids.kiddle.co/Michelangelo.

"Michelangelo, His Sculptures and Paintings." *Michelangelo: Paintings, Sculptors, Biography*. Accessed June 2022. https://www.michelangelo.org/.

"Michelangelo's Pieta." *ItalianRenaissance.org*. 2015. http://www.italianrenaissance.org/michelangelos-pieta/.

"Middle Ages: The Black Death Plague." *Ducksters*. Technological Solutions, Inc. 2022. www.ducksters.com/history/middle_ages_black_death.php.

"Niccolo Machiavelli." *Academic Kids Encyclopedia*. Accessed June 2022. https://www.academickids.com/encyclopedia/index.php/Niccolo_Machiavelli.

"Niccolò Machiavelli." *Stanford Encyclopedia of Philosophy*. Last updated May 2019. https://plato.stanford.edu/entries/machiavelli/.

"Nicolaus Copernicus Facts for Kids." *Kiddle Encyclopedia*. Last modified 19 March 2022. https://kids.kiddle.co/Nicolaus_Copernicus.

"Petrarch Facts for Kids." *Kiddle Encyclopedia*. Last modified 19 March 2022. https://kids.kiddle.co/Petrarch.

"Petrus Ramus." *Stanford Encyclopedia of Philosophy*. Last updated October 2022. https://plato.stanford.edu/entries/ramus/.

"Philosophical Skepticism Facts for Kids." *Kiddle Encyclopedia*. Last modified 9 April 2022. https://kids.kiddle.co/Philosophical_skepticism.

"Pope Julius II Facts for Kids." *Kiddle Encyclopedia*. Last modified 19 March 2022. https://kids.kiddle.co/Pope_Julius_II.

"Pope Leo X (Giovanni de' Medici)." *The Medici Family*. Accessed June 2022. http://www.themedicifamily.com/Pope-Leo-X.html.

"Renaissance." *Britannica Kids*. Encyclopedia Britannica. Accessed May 2022. https://kids.britannica.com/kids/article/Renaissance/353705#.

"Renaissance Architecture." *Academic Kids Encyclopedia*. Accessed June 2022. https://academickids.com/encyclopedia/index.php/Renaissance_architecture.

"Renaissance: Architecture and Buildings." *Ducksters*. Technological Solutions, Inc. 2022. https://www.ducksters.com/history/renaissance_architecture.php.

"Renaissance Architecture Facts for Kids." *Kiddle Encyclopedia*. Last modified 9 April 2022. https://kids.kiddle.co/Renaissance_architecture.

"Renaissance Facts for Kids." *Kiddle Encyclopedia*. Last modified 16 July 2021. https://kids.kiddle.co/Renaissance.

"Renaissance: Medici Family." *Ducksters*. Technological Solutions, Inc. 2022. https://www.ducksters.com/history/renaissance/medici_family.php.

"Renaissance Philosophy." *Academic Kids Encyclopedia*. Accessed June 2022. https://academickids.com/encyclopedia/index.php/Renaissance_philosophy.

"Renaissance: Science and Inventions." *Ducksters*. Technological Solutions, Inc. 2022. https://www.ducksters.com/history/renaissance_science.php.

"Rene Descartes." *Academic Kids Encyclopedia*. Accessed June 2022.
https://academickids.com/encyclopedia/index.php/Rene_Descartes.

"René Descartes Facts for Kids." *Kiddle Encyclopedia*. Last modified 19 March 2022.
https://kids.kiddle.co/Ren%C3%A9_Descartes.

"Sir Isaac Newton Biography for Kids." *Sir Isaac Newton Online*. 2022.
http://sirisaacnewton.info/sir-isaac-newton-biography/sir-isaac-newton-biography-kids/.

"Skepticism." *Academic Kids Encyclopedia*. Accessed May 2022.
https://academickids.com/encyclopedia/index.php/Sceptic.

"The Influence of the Renaissance." *St. John's College*. Univeristy of Cambridege.
Accessed June 2022. https://www.joh.cam.ac.uk/library/influence-
renaissance#:~:text=The%20population%20was%20becoming%20wealthier,scientifi
c%20discoveries%20and%20new%20inventions.

"The Palazzo Vecchio Museum and Tower." *Visit Florence*. Accessed June 2022.
https://www.visitflorence.com/florence-monuments/palazzo-vecchio.html.

"The Renaissance: How Did It Begin?" *Ducksters*. Technological Solutions, Inc. 2022.
https://www.ducksters.com/history/how_did_the_renaissance_start.php.

"The Renaissance Facts for Kids." *History for Kids*. Generate Press. 2022.
https://historyforkids.org/renaissance/.

Tillman, Nola Taylor. "Nicolaus Copernicus Biography: Facts and Discoveries."
Space.com. Future US Inc. 17 January 2022.

Made in the USA
Las Vegas, NV
08 May 2024